Taking Your

Camera to

INDIA

Ted Park

www.steck-vaughn.com

Published by Raintree Steck-Vaughn Publishers,
an imprint of Steck-Vaughn Company

Library of Congress Cataloging-in-Publication Data is available upon request

Printed in the United States of America
10 9 8 7 6 5 4 3 2 1 W 03 02 01 00

Cover photo: Taj Mahal

Photo acknowledgments
Cover ©Telegraph Colour Library/FPG International; p.1 ©Kugler, Jean/FPG International; p.3a ©VCG/FPG International; p.3b ©Kugler, Jean/FPG International; p.3c ©Jeremy Ferguson/Global Gypsy Photography; p.3d ©Pet, Paul/FPG International; p.4 ©Kugler, Jean/FPG International; p.5 ©VCG/FPG International; pp.8, 9, 11 ©Jeremy Ferguson/Global Gypsy Photography; pp.12, 13 ©Telegraph Colour Library/FPG International; p.14 ©VCG/FPG International; p.15 ©Jeremy Ferguson/Global Gypsy Photography; p.17 ©Zurek, Nikolay/FPG International; p.19 ©Pet, Paul/FPG International; p.20 ©Kugler, Jean/FPG International; p.21 ©Jeremy Ferguson/Global Gypsy Photography; p.23 ©Kugler, Jean/FPG International; p.24 ©Jeremy Ferguson/Global Gypsy Photography; pp.25, 26 ©Jean Kugler, FPG International; p.28a ©Kugler, Jean/FPG International; pp.28b, 29a ©Jeremy Ferguson/Global Gypsy Photography; p.29b ©Telegraph Colour Library/FPG International.

Contents

 # You're in India!

India is a large country located in Asia and it has very different kinds of land. There are tall, snow-capped mountains, thick jungles and a desert called the **Thar**.

India has several interesting cities. Many of them are very large. The city of New Delhi was built when the British ruled India, from the 1700s until 1947. The

Mumbai or Bombay is known as the "Gateway to India" because it is one of the largest and fastest cities.

If you ever visit the Thar Desert, you will probably see it while riding a camel. Because it is so large and hot, a guide must travel with you.

new city was built next to the old city of Delhi. New Delhi is the capital of India. **Bangalore** is another large city in India and is located in the south of India.

India is so big that in different parts of the country people have different religions and languages. They also have special foods and dress. In some areas, people live the way they have lived for thousands of years. In other areas, people live in towering skyscrapers.

This book will show you some of the best things about India. You will learn interesting things about the country and the people who live there. So, when you're ready to take your camera there, you'll know exactly what to do and where to go. Enjoy your trip!

# Looking at the Land

India is the seventh largest country in the world. It is about 2,000 miles (3,218 km) north to south and is about 1,822 miles (2,933 km) from east to west. In area, India is 1,269,340 square miles (3,287,590 sq km). This makes it about one-third the size of the United States.

India has the second largest population. China is the only country that has more people. Almost one-fifth of the world's population lives in India. This is believed to be just over 1 billion people.

India has many neighbors. These countries include Pakistan, Nepal, Bhutan, Myanmar (once known as Burma), Bangladesh, and China.

India is part of an area sometimes known as a **subcontinent**. This means the area is not truly a continent, but it is as large as some continents. In fact, long ago India was a piece of continent that drifted north and crashed into Asia. People who study the Earth believe this created the **Himalaya** Mountains.

India is roughly in the shape of a diamond.

PAKISTAN

Islamabad ★

JAMMU
AND
KASHMIR

LADAKH RANGE

Indus

New Delhi ★

THAR DESERT

Ganges

Agra

NEPAL

Kathmandu ★

HIMALAYA RANGE

Salween

BHUTAN

★Thimphu

Brahmaputra

Mekong

Jinsha R.

Varanasi

Ganges

BANGLADESH

Dhaka

Ganges

Calcutta

INDIA

MYANMAR

N
W ● E
S

Bombay ● Pune

DECCAN PLATEAU

Salween R.

★Rangoon

Bangalore ●

● Madras

KERALA

TAMIL
NADU

INDIA

—— International Boundary
★ National Capital
—— River
▲ Mountain

0   500 Miles

0   500 Kilometers

SRI LANKA

★Colombo

7 📷

These men make their living catching fish in the Bay of Bengal.

Its northern point is in the Himalaya Mountains. These mountains are some of the tallest in the world. They stretch about 1,500 miles (2,413 km) across northern India.

Just south of the Himalayas is the north Indian Plain. This area is also known as Hindustan. South of Hindustan is a **plateau**, known as the **Deccan**. A plateau is a flat area of land that is higher than the land around it. The Deccan is about 2,000 feet (610 m) above sea level. Sea level is the average level of the surface of the ocean. It is the starting point from which to measure the height or depth of any place.

India's large size causes weather to be very different from one region to the next. In the north, it may snow.

In the south, temperatures can climb as high as 114°F.

Windstorms blow during the summer from the southwest. These winds, known as monsoons, bring needed heavy rains. Most of the rain in India comes from the monsoons. There are cyclones in the eastern part of the country. Cyclones bring heavy rains that can cause floods.

The Himalayan Mountains extend into three regions of India: Jammu, Kashmir and Ladakh. Ladakh is known for its beautiful snow-capped mountains.

# Calcutta

Calcutta is India's second largest city, after **Mumbai** (also known as Bombay). Almost 12 million people live in Calcutta. It is a major port city. Calcutta is located on the Hooghly River, which is part of the **Ganges** delta. A delta is a triangular piece of land where a river empties into a larger body of water.

Calcutta has grown very quickly in the last 50 years. This is mainly because people have moved into the city from the countryside to look for better jobs. Calcutta is very crowded. It is also a major center for small industries.

Calcutta has a famous park named the Maidan. There are drives, gardens, and playing fields in the park. Nearby are many beautiful homes. In 1986 India's first subway system opened in Calcutta.

While in Calcutta, don't forget to visit the Victoria Memorial. It was first built to honor the British Empire. It is now a museum.

 # Great Places to Visit

**This is the Taj Mahal. The main part of the monument is made
entirely of white marble.**

The first place you should visit is the **Taj Mahal**. It
is a building in **Agra**. It is made almost completely out
of white marble. It was built between 1632 and 1667.

The building is Shah Jahan's memorial to his wife, who died during childbirth. It took about 22,000 people about fifteen years to build the Taj Mahal. Every year people come from all over the world to see this amazing building.

Another place to visit is Varanasi. It is a special city in the northeast of India. It is special because it is located on the Ganges River, which is considered sacred to most Indian people. The river is so important that many people have their ashes scattered in the Ganges after they die.

The city of Varanasi is a holy place in India. These people are bathing in the Ganges River because many Indians believe that it is sacred.

The People

The Indus River and its valley were the home of the first people of India.

India is made up of many ethnic groups. An ethnic group is made up of people who share features such as language, religion, or customs. Two of India's largest ethnic groups are the Hindi and the Bengali.

These women are wearing traditional dance costumes.

For many years India had a **caste system**. A caste is a group or social class. A person's caste determined his or her place in the community and the job a person might have. People had to stay in the castes they were born into. They could not marry a person who was from a different caste or receive the same education. Some people did not belong to any

The women in this fishing village are wearing saris (*sah-ree*), the traditional clothing worn in India by women.

caste. They were known as untouchables. The untouchables belonged to the lowest social class in India. The caste system was outlawed when India became independent in 1947.

Hindi and English are the two most spoken languages in India. Hindi is one of the official languages of India. There are more than 16 other national languages, and at least 1,600 **dialects**. A dialect is a different way of speaking the same language.

 # How Do People Live in India?

People in India often have big families. Generally, all of the members of a family live together. Families often have many children.

Dogs, cats, chickens, and goats often ride the crowded trains and buses with their owners. Sometimes people ride on top of these vehicles because there is no room inside. Many people ride bicycles or motor bikes with sidecars. Families often carry their own food when they travel, along with small stoves on which to cook.

Only 20 percent of Indians live in cities. One-fifth of these people live in poverty. They may live on the streets or in shanties made from cardboard or scrap metal. The power often goes off and sometimes there is not enough water. Many people don't have clean water to drink.

Most of the population live in small villages. Some

 16

experts believe there may be as many as 600,000 villages in India. The houses in these villages are often made of clay, stone, or brick. Sometimes the houses are built around small courtyards. A courtyard is a open area surrounded by walls.

What a traffic jam! Have you ever seen a camel in the middle of the road? This is a perfect time to take a picture.

Government and Religion

Government

India is a **republic** and a member of the British Commonwealth of Nations. It is the world's largest democracy. It is a union of 25 states and 7 union territories. These 7 territories include islands off the coast and some of the larger cities.

India's Parliament is divided into two groups, an upper and lower house. Together, these groups make India's laws. Members of Parliament are elected by a vote of the people. Members of Parliament elect the president for a five-year term. The president picks a prime minister, who runs the country.

Religion

Eight out of ten Indians are Hindus. In the **Hindu religion** there are many gods. Each god has a favorite animal. Animals are very important to Hindus. You will

 18

see many animals, mainly cows, walking freely around the cities and towns of India. People will touch the forehead of the cow for good luck.

Other religions in India include **Sikhism**, Christianity, **Buddhism** and **Islam**. People who follow the Islam religion are known as Muslims. One percent of Indians are Buddhists.

The famous Kapaleeshwara temple is located in Madras. It is dedicated to one of the Hindu gods. This would make a great picture!

Earning a Living

About half of the Indian people are farmers. Most of the work is done by hand. Farmers grow rice in the southeastern part of the country. Wheat is grown in the north. Other major crops include tobacco, cotton and jute. Jute is a plant used to make canvas and cloth mats. Some tents are made out of canvas.

India has many natural resources. The most important are iron ore, bauxite and copper ore. Iron ore is made into steel. Bauxite is used for aluminum. Many of these resources are used in industry.

This merchant sells brightly-colored jewelry, clothing and other items to both Indians and people visiting the country.

These women are picking tea in the southern state of Kerala.

Industries in India include steel, machinery, chemicals, and computer software. Often businesses are small and run by families.

In Mumbai (Bombay), there is a large movie industry, where 800 films are made each year. Indian films are shown all around the world.

Along the coasts of India, fishing is important. Small old-fashioned boats can be seen alongside modern boats.

# School and Sports

School

Education is very important. The school day is hard. In some places students work on computers and the Internet. In other schools, however, students use small chalkboards for their lessons. In other places, books and paper are very scarce. Scarce means something is hard to find because there is so little of it.

When school is finished, many Indian children are expected to return home to work on the family farm or business. But some go to college. About 12,000 medical students graduate each year. Many of these people leave India after they graduate, because there are not enough jobs for everyone.

Sports

Cricket is a popular sport in India. Cricket is a game that the English people introduced to India when they ruled. It is a game like baseball but it is played with a flat bat.

 22

Education is very important in India. These children are enjoying a beautiful day while learning.

 # Food and Holiday Fun

Indian food is often spicy and is enjoyed by many people all over the world.

Let's Eat!

Many Indians like to use curry to give flavor to their cooking. Curry is a blend of many different spices. Because of religious beliefs, many Indians are vegetarians. This means they don't eat meat. Indians often take the food and roll it into pieces of flat bread that are known as **chapatis**.

People in different parts of India eat different kinds

 24

of foods. Indians usually don't use knives and forks, but instead use bread and their fingers.

Celebrate!

Most celebrations in India are connected with the Hindu religion. Holi is a holiday at the end of winter that celebrates the coming of spring. In October or November, Hindus celebrate the festival of lights known as Divali. It lasts for five days. During this time, Hindus clean their homes, light oil lamps, exchange candies, and set off fireworks. It is a noisy and colorful holiday.

Elephants are decorated for many events. The elephant is a special animal to many Indians because it represents one of the Hindu gods.

25 📷

The Future

If you took your camera to India, you would see a country that has changed in many ways. There are still problems that India has not solved. Living conditions, food, water, medical care, population control, and education are all areas India is working hard to improve. India has the kinds of problems that many large

countries have. There is a lot of poverty. Only about half of all Indians can read and write.

The damage that has been done to India's environment is a big problem that Indians are working hard to solve. They are planting new trees so that there will be more forests. Indians have set aside large pieces of land as national parks, where different kinds of plants and animals can live safely.

The people of India care a great deal about their country. And they are working to make it an even better place.

When you leave India, a person may speak to you in Hindi. They may say "*namaste*" (nah-MAS-tay), which means good-bye in English.

◀ **The India Gate in New Delhi was built to honor soldiers who fought for their country.**

Quick Facts About INDIA

Capital ▶
New Delhi

Borders
Pakistan, China, Nepal, Bhutan,
Myanmar, Bangladesh

Area
1,269,300 square miles
(3,286,067 sq km)

Population
1,014,003,817

Largest Cities
Mumbai (Bombay) 17,850,000
Calcutta (Kolkata) 12,900,000

Chief crops
rice, grains, sugar cane, spices, tea,
cashews, cotton, potatoes, jute,
oilseed

Natural resources
coal, iron ore, manganese, mica,
bauxite, titanium ore, chromite,
diamonds, natural gas, petroleum,
limestone

Longest river
Ganges: 1,560 miles (2,510 km)

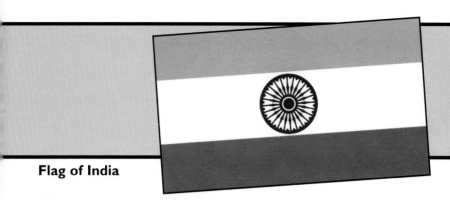

Flag of India

◀ **Coastline**
3,533 miles (5,686 km)

Monetary unit
rupee

Literacy rate
52 percent of Indians can read and write.

Major industries
textiles, steel, processed foods, cement, machinery, chemicals, mining, transportation equipment, petroleum

Glossary

Agra: (AH-gra) The city where the Taj Mahal is located.

Bangalore: (BANG-a-lor) A large city in southern India that is built on a ridge.

Buddhism: (BOO-diz-uhm) A religion that follows the teachings of Buddha.

Calcutta: (cal-CUT-a) The second largest city in India and a major port.

Caste system: (KAST SISS-tem) A way of keeping people divided into classes.

Chapatis: (chuh-PAH-thees) A flat whole wheat bread.

Deccan: (DEH-kuhn) A plateau in India, south of Hindustan.

Dialect: (DYE-uh-lekt) A way a language is spoken in a particular place or among a group of people.

Divali: (dee-VAH-lee) The festival of lights, a holiday when Hindus clean their homes, light oil lamps, exchange candies, and set off fireworks.

Ganges: (GANE-jez) A holy river in India.

Himalayas: (him-uh-LAY-uhs) A range of mountains that are among the tallest in the world.

 30

Hindi: (HIN-dee) An official language of India.

Hindu religion: (HIN-doo ree-LI-jun) A religion where animals are seen as sacred so they are not harmed.

Holi: (HOH-lee) A Hindu holiday that celebrates the coming of spring.

Indus River Valley: (IN-dus RIV-ur VAL-ee) The home of the first people who lived in India.

Islam: (i-SLAHM) A religion that follows the teachings of Mohammed.

Mumbai: (MUM-by) The largest city in India and home to India's film industry.

Plateau: (pla-TOH) An area of high, flat land.

Republic: (ri-PUHB-lik) A form of government where the people have the power to elect those who will run the government.

Sikhism: (SEEK-is-um) A religion in India whose members believe it is important to take care of others.

Subcontinent: (suhb-KON-tuh-nuhnt) An area that is not truly a continent, but that is as large as some continents.

Taj Mahal: (TAHJ mah-HALL) A memorial made entirely of white marble.

Thar: (TAHR) A desert in western India.

Index